C0-ARJ-830

More praise for *lesser case*

For years I have been reading DeCarteret's work, watching him peel away at the layers of truth and reality one book at a time. In *lesser case*, perhaps his best, he has hit on the nerve of the Self. Here he puts the Self and the World through a sieve until he distills all of the ruses. Even the ruse of his own writing. Thus speaking for all of us. Are there shades of Frost's dark nights in these poems? Yes. Perhaps the Frost that sits down for drinks with Baudelaire and Rimbaud. For there is that sweet touch of humor and decadence in here too. Don't believe anything Mark said in his previous 6 works. Believe everything in this one.

— **S Stephanie**, Author of *So This Is What It Has Come To*

Mallarmé's symbolism invoked early on, DeCarteret's poems speak of a life spent in conversation with the self and other poets. The poems weave themselves, tease out meaning the more you read them. Anagrams constantly talking back to themselves, they honor as they grieve for poets and poetry. Genius segues link these poems' motifs, hold them up to the light: from window to water, sun to flame, pen to tongue, words and wordlessness, paper crumpled, balled up like asterisks, webs to madness to mazes. They are the lack as much as the purposefully left blank. These poems will make you pay attention – to elements, ghosts and chairs – reckon with religion. The poet's trick, "throwing one's latest voice", tricks the poet. Marrying language with meaning. Leaving punctuation to ampersands, question marks, and slashes, the line break is the modus operandi. Not a period in sight, the poet ends *lesser case* with itches still left to scratch. They reach the reader, who might be holy if they would make the poet whole.

— **Jessica Purdy**, Author of *Sleep in a Strange House*

lesser case

MARK DECARTERET

Nixes Mate Books
Allston, Massachusetts

Copyright © 2021 Mark DeCarteret

Book design by d'Entremont
Cover photograph

All rights reserved. This book or any portion thereof may not be
reproduced or used in any manner whatsoever without the express
written permission of the publisher except for the use of brief quotations
in a book review or scholarly journal.

ISBN 978-1-949279-30-6

Nixes Mate Books
POBox 1179
Allston, MA 02134
nixesmate.pub

in memory of Sam Cornish

thanks, more than ever, to Kathleen

Contents

lesser case

front

where my shaking finds company
more light has gone bad
& yet the weary recognitions
always happily remain

how I know in the case
of the Bib-n-Crib
the shop's sign was in existence
ages before the store

& how at this stage I would do
just about anything for anything
& to think I always thought
I was resolute or this readymade

first we had bed creaks
& all sorts of hunger
then reality sat in even
more radiant aberrations

unread

I cram old roses down into a barrel
w/a borrowed book of Mallarmé
in this year of no controversy
once again a changed man

the mirror offers suggestions –
should somebody talk the sun
away from the window *Does*
Pride at evening always fume?

but the self reassures us of nothing
nor the blood & its storylines
only what one has left to be done w/
has little or no thought of leaving

her spun sugared blurs

these scissors have seen to
outliving almost all of my epics:
those lives that have lapsed on the page
always bent on some symmetry

how can anyone relax in this house anymore?
a glass of water that was meant to be
drunk hours earlier keeps putting me in mind
of the place on the window where the bird had struck

then the pencil trying to arrive at another world
where my past is not printed alongside its spine
w/its hauntings having taken what life I had left:
seems twice now I'll have forfeited these dreams

hindrance

hair everywhere
sounded by tongue
& rethought by fingers

place this unfinished
poem w/those other
unfinished books yes

more of Valery's tic
lost somewhere at sea
& the cat as it smirks

its scent on the page
so now you must
baptize this pen

& its holder
for even when a word
suggests silver

there will still be
much more of me
acquainted w/silence

helium

she still keeps a balloon
he filled up his last birthday
& every year since
takes in one of his breaths
& makes this similar wish

host

going in I had known
for it's one thing to
go in for a week or two
another as a god

you'd cooed at parts
I'd left starred
your lips shaping
the air like a temple

later this green light
emerged out new snow
not so much getting
in between the world

& the page but
the gap & the word
I had thought I'd
weaned off of it

I have a minor in visual arts

& the same torpor & rope burns
reported here last time
also the sky left intentionally blank
& some fallen blossoms, half-buds

I looked up the missed details
& all that my notebook seemed to lack
when I took it up the night before last
while under the tanning bed, drinking

so useless at riding a half-decent line
but brings its own highlighter, whiteout
to where those stars were once slung
& the gunshot couldn't reach us

now those starlings I once rated
an 8 are not even worth
throwing one's latest voice –
that shock of hearing one

making a lesser case for oneself
those options topping off at age ten
when all that was new could be
spotted from right here on the lake

so what's not to liken to anything else?
each modification a blow of sorts
leaving me wobbly as a calf
licked well past relevance

inhabitants

this is why they
won't allow us

to throw our hats
onto the bed

or eat dinner
on our own

our hands all
but these hearts

the windows more
me than anyone

or even say who it
was we'd rerouted

led out from this
shadowed wall

& nearly thawed
in the wood-heat

red to our eyes
w/the wonder

a feeling here down
where the wind's at

we won't ever be
worthy of this house

instrumental

w/each breath
I am sucked in again
though it always claimed nothing
rhymed w/it but din
or the heart as it burrowed in
deeper & finally deep

like the last time I'd let lion
have a line to its self
proof that I had begun once again
to uproot all its secrets
step over me please
we are nothing more than elbows & knees

& me w/my swashbuckler's pen
clenched between these falsest of teeth
I am only attached to the world
by the words it has tried keeping from me
dead leaves cupping water
or tissues mangled into blossom

my feet reluctant to take me anywhere
when neither can agree on my history
a janitor's mop barring the entrance
to paradise's longest sleep over
the only mercy I've been shown is the wind's
& that one difficult note that's played over & over

again

the itinerary of shade

once opening my mouth
so had begun the sun's day

once put to paper
I tried finishing off the sun w/my eyes

once I came back to no windows
after lending out my room to the sun & its offspring

once leaving the river
the sun could be seen in most everything

once I read so much into the light
the sun up & swallowed me whole

iv

at long last the tongue has surrendered
to the flame's latest take on infinity

the holes which had once promised song
now let me see clear through to bone

get me somebody good w/a scalpel
get me somebody good w/a light

how the crocodile king dons its carousel crown
all those fears of mine finally made flesh

I am drug free I am drug free I am drug free
I am drug free I am drug free I am drug free

much rather the dry heave of wordlessness
than the excruciating measure of this

just

far enough into the forest
there's the sound of this nuthatch

clean as laughing gas
activated w/fall's light

I will try channeling later
when I take chalk to slate

as if it foretells of a letting-up
of all the snow we have seen to

& now relive a hundred fold
w/the favor of a candle

the kingfisher

to Charles Olson

once the blue flame
had caught in my throat –
a hundred years of having cross-
walked through the thorn & the turbine
indoctrinated w/every wind's whim
dribbled out on my bib
in a luxurious rust:
not one death but many
the sun the same failure
that some golden age once had tested for
while out in the courtyard
w/their knees bruised & bent
so exquisitely backwards
a sentence they eventually survive
w/eyedroppers of mettle & irony
I hunt among stones
where the shadows have long been
trying to enter their side of our story

the last ever ode to one's pencil

even w/the sky full of sun, unflawed
I'll waffle or low-ball, tell you lies

go what you've come to call
post-modernist on you

try to sell you on the same sparrow
I saw yesterday atop the potted flowers

(was I ever that open, to-the-point?
I'd have to opine, nope, probably not)

& now spot out this window
white-capped & dun, falling through space

risking the existence of this chair
rows of books worried into maze

in my lab coat & paper hat
as I ball up more poems into asterisks*

*please know if I'm lost on you, stolen & sold-off-in-lots,
 that my line about love was about a lot more than just votes

last up

deserted silo
harangued by the sun
though the head's
long gone soft
w/more gods
than the sky knows
what to do w/

once his hands
had rummaged
through the world's
darkest quarters
now they peel back
some wrap
on some food
a black cat leaving
more fits of dust
on the delivery truck's hood

a red arrow
only on half the time
more this questionable light
just off in the distance

he's stopped moving
his mouth long enough
for the world to know
he hasn't any answers

launch

morning & an
admission of sorts
a sky simulcast
cloud & more cloud
then a line about
figuring somehow
this horse's birthday
that I supply most the bliss
betrayed by the performance

minutes fight for more
breaths while the seconds
mostly shrug & suggest

we are stunned by expectations
into playthings something lacquered
hearing all sorts of claims here
how someone once a king
& another sharpened teeth
on what little light
had been spoken

line break

sure when I
cross myself

blur egg on
my face

you're so quick
to turn a phrase

but now look
at your loss

for words
when I ask you

where my hands were
just then?

lord god bird

no matter how
long I kept at it
your negative
never amounted
to very much –
not unlike
looking into the sun
if one holds their
place long enough
one will begin
to see the ghosts
burning their way
back into things

metaphysics

I axed the air
for a way out
being that I balk
at most anything
brown or balled up
as I'm walking
around & around –
the slightest of slips
& the letters will
go all unsounded
recalling a song
sung by only one
lip or a light
beyondbrightness
I squint at
& equate to
more time
I keep talking
myself through

missal

here time's syringe
slips under the skin
loading us down
w/more sleep
the eyes closed
telling us more
than we need know
how only one thing is sure
in the course of the day
our blood will only
serve those gods
we've worn down most
to our own image

mt Washington (march)

I had fallen in w/that line
where no amount at times

wasn't looked at as so low
so shadow dash snow

musclebound

even the stars have been evacuated
so let's dispense w/the formality
of resigning ourselves to these postage
stamped interiors & euphemisms
for soon our defeat will put an end
to those questionings – who left on the fan
or ate crackers too close to the transistor?
the red flag is its own destination
& the wind's always been parenthetical
its tissue-thin opinions near par w/this
flower's flimsiest of debaucheries

soon you'll talk only in secretive signs –
look again it says nothing but hands!
& our past but a diabolical locket

you had me evicted so long ago
they only say it's so easy going on like this
as if having at it w/both our minds
would equate to some kinder occupation
so I'm shelving the idea about death being flight

& flight being the fact of my matter irreparable
instead writing myself into the story where
for most touch is nuisance – more time
to be spent removed from the feed

mused

early on I was claimed by the talentless as their saint
because I'd taken beauty to be a sort of airy task, lacking

I'd have you listen to a recording of a doorbell
while mail ordering stills of the lit-from-behind

below the catwalk from an overhead cam you'd see
what looked like a web tacked to the make-believe lawn

I was really more of a latent daycare giver
w/a bias towards easy-baked miracles, scare-tactics

what wasn't dun-hued was sun-damaged
as I made yet another game out of madness

next to this country

here the dead orbit us
& most everything whistles
except for the teetering pines
& the ducks cut from paper

no two ever say it the same though
they have come close in the middle
where the maze takes on heat
& they are making believe they can hack it

I'm not a supper person per se
but I may have been swayed by what glaze
they've slapped onto the bird
so much like the sun lowering onto my chin all aglow

while you are one w/the dust & the dung
a shotgun hyphened at your chest
the leaves rusty & taken w/death
as you breathe in more matter

I am finished w/truth
& how it tastes to my tongue
of philosopher's busts
& light so antiquated it shuns us

here I am speaking of it in a photograph
as well as the lack left by laughter & drinks
like the splash come to ice
that next mishap

sure its past can be taken up
each moment worried into a plea
whose memory is a wheel &
whose flag's still a blank

night

nothing
more
to be
made
of any
of it

ode to antarctica

yeah south of south
snow & cold & all that
so happy how we mouth
your formations lowest land
maybe you have penguins
& the light playing
all by its lonesome

ode to the unopened notebook

it's mostly me adlibbing, unbilled –
page after page of pain management
the rain or the air not yet there
neither good at lying nor siding w/me

a lap dog's been keeping my place
where I went in all post-modernist
& came out this rockabilly act
sharing the stage w/another half-rate poet

I can't get my legs out of my jeans
I can't get the gel out of my hair
it was that rarest of eras – some staring
at the stars, some helping themselves

the once untamable season

the hallway blocked w/suspicious boxes
no longer the standard remiss
the audible range of the snowmobile
stresses the blurt of shaggy sirens
o helper so further in terms of God farther!
the verdigris palm reconstructed, held alive
by a clock's ruse & the seminally converted
what could be meant by all these indexes?
the locked heart speaks of only forever

of graves & graffiti

one hundred years hence
& we'll still be awaiting
the rain we've long needed

u smashed up or what?

the weather's never ending
even if we dismissed the whole sky
what clouds would these mouths not pursue?

boy this acid is great

the schoolhouse got bloed up
both the Dickinson boys & their cousins
taken down to be fitted for wings

I don't feel for nobody

one will work as well as the other

hot like those locusts come unstuck in my skull
the look of the sun snapped back into place

& cold like the lock on the old barn door
the unbidden click of its numbers

over (come)

so far
we have blown
without having found
that one note
or the stones
which we gathered
would help us
get a read
on our hearts
& though the sound
of our bodies
seems to have
more in common
w/silence –
that hushed report
of time –
we have not once
been alone
or not near
what we'd hoped
to fall under

paraskevidekatriaphobia

I put down a chair
where there wasn't one
& then welcome more distance

starlings suffocate my call
so all you'll know of any snow
will come to you from the sky

for the next world bring only your back
or anything that you've stolen
& breathed into w/night

a vulture chick circles
its throat all aflame
& its heart filled w/hunger

I think back to my mother
her winter boots capsized w/blood
& my tiny fists lit from within

what will the wind have to say
of the new grass & calm?
what does any past want w/recovery?

I'm glad it is you & not the hornets again
somewhere I hope they pay good
money for these tricks of mine

pay heaven (no mind)

o divine grind of teeth
& blessed asterisk!
Jesus pays no mind
to most of my sins
o the mischief I got in
once someone had
mistaken my brace
for a playing piece
that bird out back's
been trying to put me
in a trance again
& if the sun sits just right
& the window's all light
maybe Jesus does slip
later into slots where
the stars had been
w/my tongue half-convincing
me to lie to Him again
re: the unintelligible dance

of which my name's
become recently tied
that I've already sampled
in another poem some-
where a different mistake

(minor) prophecy

mercy's flag at long last
the world helping itself
to your memories again
I grope for the last of the chairs
while a ghost tries explaining
the stains on the floor
would it help me
to remember you speaking
how you held to my bones
like the closest of casts
& why was it I'd raced
from one purchase to the next
as night went off surrendering
so many of its blossoms
more decals for what
when no one knows we are here
yet I'll borrow more blood
as I await that rarest
kind of perception
punched out from the light

practice

to Bill Knott

lately I'm good for maybe
five or six lines
then ellipses:
these tiniest of stones
reminding me
how the poet in front of
the white page
always makes for
the most obvious of targets

puppet show

that woodpecker should
get itself a new wreck –
a toy w/more fuel in it
less flesh & blood, ploy

rather

than do away
w/the self
I have felt less
an interest

I talked up
the air again
till we were paired
in our lack of a calling

& then took up
our lot w/the rain
till it fell in black droplets
as if it a kind of ink

later hating
the velvety kings
we'd become
thinking ourselves

all but invisible
as our hair was combed
back in the mirror
by yet another

review: a poem

push both your eyes
back into your head
& begin again –
this unmistakable sun!
& these birds visiting
your tongue w/
questions for which
you will never be
the answer
like what if
when the wind
finally died
you had regained
your voice
but only your voice
& when the wind died
the mailbox remained
but only gutted
so that say

a plastic bag stabbed
by a branch
might rid us of guilt
remind us mid-
sentence to try
to be kinder
be kinder

sea

before it
was the sea
it was only
this memory
we kept at –
too much is
always read
into what we
had tried
speaking

sign off

in honor of reality
tv I'll create
nothing that lasts
out of nothing that
lasts long live
all of us & may we
get starfucked
by whoever played
what's-their-face
on that show
we all dreamt of
having parts on
our whole life

some say (seed)

another red rush –
not so much a cardinal
crashing the scrub

singing & stammering
cross-tongued but
branches signing

their iciest of scripts –
a blanket of wet
& then chatter, exaltation

this response to be cashed in –
an image in shambles again
like a berry's taxed memory

soul-letting

burnt out on boy-tribes & runts
more of those most remote stories

the best this the best that
lists of celebrity photoshop tips

(here I'll skip to some country minus
phoned-in e-pics & simulcast sunsets)

as well as creatures aping men
& men caped always packing

or orbiting yet another toy sun
their rockets oft-gunned but untested, stunted

southern exposure

reinforcements added up to
an almost rain almost snow
& me doubling over in worship again

w/this refrain that had
long turned from meaning –
any thoughts of the sun angling in

& blowing the sky into epic
dismissed w/this air kiss
that light I can listen to while

checking the window for injury
my breath though expiring still
bent on betraying my body's secrets

star reading

let us wait till
that same star
turns up again, dear –
reddish & short-lived
yet rerun across the sky –
our two wishes burned off
but the both of us still here
lit up like this newest sun
wed to only what's
technically dead

strip

here where stone
turns to verse
then sometimes
back to stone
the smallest
of details
have been lost
on me &
this cursed sun
crept over
w/fog &
if anything's
believed it
is this I
I have logged
along w/
piles of shells
flounder &
an old ghost's

omniscient
blinking
where I was
called back into
this world
where some leaf
I had stuck
to the roof
of my mouth
spoke volumes
of rivers
never returning
any favors
then nothing
that nothing
like something
so unlike you
this is all
you have left
to go on

stupidest blues

now everyone walks on
the water
& dishes more out
now everyone walks
on the water
& does whatever it is
they wanted to do
so don't go & sing me
those stupidest blues
don't lie to me
no don't lie
stupidest blues
the earth will never
die never

surrender

to the luck of any god
dressed in nothing but the sheet
you have slept your entire life

then go down as no good
into the pit of yourself
stripped of all wonder

I read where the skull of Vitalis
patron saint of genital disease
will be selling at auction today

we'll stick a red tab
where the flower had been
cut for your induction

a dozen or so doves
let back into the sky
versed in little but light

time slot

nothing hungry to feed
& nothing further to protest
I look for something soft
to run my fingers through

that unspeakable hour

to Gary Widger

noon & the clouds collide

noon & some sun but not
eyed or even owed its own line

noon went on & on & on, no?

noon there's more hell
in the telling of it

noon I won't abide in your chill anymore

noon I'm no longer emboldened
by my own sighs or anyone else's

noon because your light's such a hard sell

noon & gone is the frost
that interpreted the world

noon it wasn't the cold that I lied

noon where I've confided
the last of my farewells

noon how my bones have always tried me

noon & I've shut my eyes
on all that I held dear

noon where even death sleeps off time

what's happened is this

air not that different than rain

some moss on the railing & stairs

a newt that went wet, wetter

so maybe a sky stopper-shut might suit me

red as a sort of blind, afterthought

I spot a rabbit, its barred sides & twitches

a blot of ink tweezed into blossom

was what I saw any different than

winter haiku

here we have five or six
different words for snow
& they all start w/fuck

anesthetic

I took off my shoes before entering
but this reassured no one
not even the dogs who were lapping
the floor dead of stars

nothing sounds better
than thoughts wet w/ink
that moment we take to the sky
knowing this last line will have to do

asterism

after the star
trailed off
as if fated
or at odds
w/the tales
all these dots
had formed
I find myself
stalled at
the railing
fattening up
on the soon-
to-die light
that leads
first into
the fields
or the forests
then later
(lied about
if any of it
is to last) –
the rafters

august

the gulls are all business
w/this century's charge

applying their hoarse benedictions
to the parking lot's shins

I take nothing from the car
leaving even my shoes at the pedals

o the calm smack of a cloud's intercession
yet more guarantees from the sea!

I bend down so as not
to stymie the sky

as if the world has been
kissed back in place

& we're known only by our skin
the heat that's taken it up as its own

b actor in a movie

maybe damned more by
these five ill-bred tercets
than Adam's binary fissions

that same bloody landmass
halved & cussed over again
where my Dad is viewing

what he believes to be
Sasquatch asking so little
of any river or sun god

as it suckles its young
fusses over its cowlick
& lack of known suffering

adding to his inner secret
agent's denture-tending
& ungainly quadrangles

blinked/blank

when my eyelids sang
of all I'd seen shadow-wise
that other life carved out of darkness
I wasn't able to listen

when my eyelids said
all that the corporate heads insisted
their fiery brands on my temple
I lost my own scent

when my eyelids sagged
into cold & colder artifact
thoughts entrenched in my skull
I could no longer feel

when my eyelids sank
& my body cramped into a cipher
a reminder of what it once played at
I became even dumber

when my eyelids saw
nothing of what they once were
only light & light's offspring
I knew all along night had dreamt me

boulevard

to Sam Cornish

he's done
more damage
is how he tells it
trying to come to
a blessed haiku
way back when
he took up
half the world
just coughing up
something
nearly rare
or back when
he thumb plugged
that oldest of rivers
& ventured that
road they say
only veers off
for the lost shoe
or packie store
or maybe back

when he would
have given up
all his Jesuses
for a mouth
full of sedans

breath

to Robert Creeley

what luck these words
knocked off like air
not to mention
the great measure
one needs to pull
off a good poem:
putting just one
of those moments
back in their place

burden

even the most aggrieved ghost
has grown fearful over time
of the relocated chair

cesarean

I had my start
at this scar where
my mother first
spoke of me
parenthetically
in between
breaths
& the half
beats we kept
to ourselves
& though my lips
were divided
over our roles
been assigned
their own
hyphen
I would still try
to talk my way
out from

that crowning
working up
these behests
from the depths
of her body
till any word
left of me
was swallowed up
nearly whole

chaos

save us I try to say
straightening up
your late aunt's vase
& putting the tulips
back in their place
the cat now tackling
a glint given off by
the skylight like this
tightest of oft-white
buds before letting that
overstrained other one –
a sprig splitting time
between our skin &
the scuffed up nicked
floors of the cottage –
really have it up till
one of us having seen
to the coffee spills &
stuffing has recovered

our voice just enough
to sound brighter more
curious than the sun

decoys

it's the animal's way of saying
you're welcome or lookee right here
at these worms made of sticks
& these deer made of sticks too

unlike when their words came in bunches
dropped like babies on the new snow
or were arranged in the sky like some
cherub w/the chubbiest of cheeks

now this one here's lit from within
while those others are bowed
their hair blown by some engine
or are each of their heads now a hat?

& next come the boats again
bringing w/them that new day
when our throats will be blest w/more vowels
& we'll sic the best of our gods on them again

dishes

whose heart
out of boredom
has not invited grief's
hammer claw?

time often mis-
steps like this
defecting to countries
long forgotten

then a draft develops
reassuring the skin
& an ant clamps itself
to the sieve again

between sometimes light
& that deepest of wells
my tongue is also torn
in its allegiances

drift

to Wallace Stevens

if only I could hold
  this breath longer
& contest the star's light
think of even one thing
not punctuated by night

at least I got the world right
if only for a minute
though it can't be a coincidence
  it happening
while I wasn't in it

earliest spring

the earth has been known
to somewhat glow this time of year
what w/the sky dismissed
the air seemingly consuming
more of itself than is advisable

we inherit little more than
the crow's blackest asterisks
thus shrugging into the concussive mist
each step less & less reluctant
to be given up by the earth

elegy

these fingers
last touched
the skin
which last touched
the bones
which will soon
touch the last
of any dirt
he'll lie still for

entertaining one's inquisitive self

just like these racks full of blank books
my thoughts have been marked down again
& given their very own mascot
who will wait for the pen's intercession
or its stomach to finally kick in again
(these factories force-feeding the heavens
breath dismissed by this blasphemous cold...)
when once I would liken these lines
to my tongue being yanked into action
now I'm clearing my throat most discreetly
any messes swiped up by the always best linen

etiquette

so little of what
he's saying
even registers

the distant eyed
glasses & smoke –
yes I can see

(what it is you are
saying) how our blessings
aren't much more

than these dry spells
folded up into perfect white
handkerchiefs

fable

I've had
no luck
finding
the forest
I was sup-
posed
to have been
lost in
forever
& ever

back (scratcher)

your littlest
plastic hand
on a stick

this itch all
I've still left
of that past

Acknowledgements

Thanks to the editors of *3rd bed, animus, Apocryphal Text, aught, Ballard Street Poetry Journal, Birds Piled Loosely, Blue Fifth Review, Brickplight, Cannot Exist, The Citron Review, foam:e, Four Corners, Gander Press Review, horse less, h_ngm_n, House Organ, Ken*again, La Petite Zine, Leaf Press, Lilliput Review, little leo journal, The Longest Day: Poems in Tribute to Gary Widger (Sargent Press), Loop, Matter, Maverick Magazine, Meat For Tea, Memorious, Mudfish, Omphalos, Otoliths, Poetry East, Poetry Super Highway, Prick of the Spindle, RiverLit, rust + moth, scissors and spackle, Segue, Spillway, Spiral Orb, Spittoon, Timber, Vinyl Poetry, welter, White Pelican Review,* & *Whole Beast Rag.*

About the Author

Mark DeCarteret has appeared next to Charles Bukowski in a lo-fi fold out, Pope John Paul II in a high-test collection of Catholic poetry, Billy Collins in an Italian fashion coffee table book, and Mary Oliver in a 3785 page pirated lit-trap.

42° 19' 47.9" N 70° 56' 43.9" W

Nixes Mate is a navigational hazard in Boston Harbor used during the colonial period to gibbet and hang pirates and mutineers.

Nixes Mate Books features small-batch artisanal literature, created by writers who use all 26 letters of the alphabet and then some, honing their craft the time-honored way: one line at a time.

nixesmate.pub

CPSIA information can be obtained
at www.ICGtesting.com
Printed in the USA
BVHW090232061121
620874BV00004B/37